T0387526

Toys

LEVEL 5

/oy/ /ie/

Teaching Tips

Green Level 5

This book focuses on the phonemes **/oy/ie/**.

Before Reading

- Discuss the title. Ask readers what they think the book will be about. Have them briefly explain why.
- Ask readers to look at the pictures and words on page 3. Sound out the words together. What other words end in "oy"?

Read the Book

- Encourage readers to break down unfamiliar words into units of sound. Then, ask them to string the sounds together to create the words.
- Urge readers to point out when the focused phonics phonemes appear in the text.

After Reading

- Encourage children to reread the book independently or with a friend.
- Ask readers to name other words with /oy/ or /ie/ phonemes. On a separate sheet of paper, have them write the words.

© 2024 Booklife Publishing
This edition is published by arrangement with Booklife Publishing.

North American adaptations © 2024 Jump!
5357 Penn Avenue South
Minneapolis, MN 55419
www.jumplibrary.com

Decodables by Jump! are published by Jump! Library.
All rights reserved. No part of this book may be reproduced in any form without written permission from the publisher.

Library of Congress Cataloging-in-Publication Data is available at www.loc.gov or upon request from the publisher.

ISBN: 979-8-88524-751-1 (hardcover)
ISBN: 979-8-88524-752-8 (paperback)
ISBN: 979-8-88524-753-5 (ebook)

Photo Credits
Images are courtesy of Shutterstock.com. With thanks to iStockphoto. Cover – anitasstudio, Prostock-studio, Inara Prusakova, Veja, Gabberr. 3 – Pixel-Shot, Mauro Rodrigues. 4&5 – shoot4pleasure, Hurst Photo, Michael Kraus, KieferPix, natalia pak. 6&7 – Aleksei Potov, Butivshchenko Olena. 8&9 – Maurotoro, Jayakri. 10&11 – R7 Photo, LightField Studios. 12&13 – Olesia Bilkei, StockPlanets. 14&15 – Hurst Photo, Lee Thompson Images, Image Source.

How many words can you think of that have an **oy** sound?

Here are two to get you started:

Boy

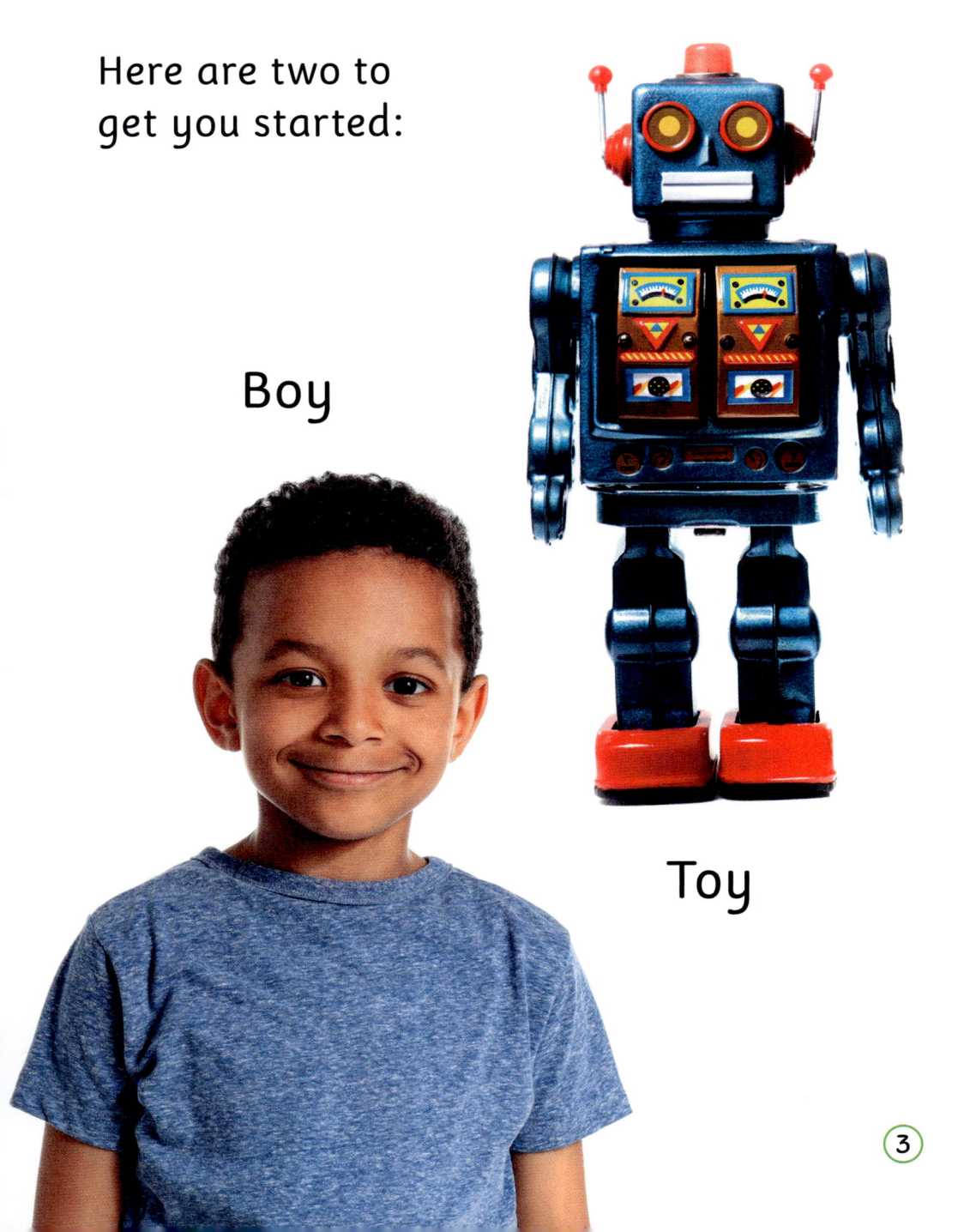

Toy

Toys are fun. There are lots of different toys to enjoy.

4

Toys to hug, toys that zoom, and toys that go up and down. What can toys do?

This toy flies up and down in the air.
Do you have a toy that flies?

It flies into a tree! The boy and his dad get the toy out.

A doll can be held in a big hug. Dolls that are soft are good for hugging.

This boy enjoys playing doctor. Dolls are fun for all kids.

You can stack wooden blocks. How high can you stack them?

It is hard to tap out the right block.
When you tap it out, add it to the top.

Toy cars are fun to play with and fix.
Toy cars can be little or big.

Roll the cars and get them to go zoom! Beep beep. Honk the horn.

Some toys can go up and down. This toy is on a string. This one has a spring.

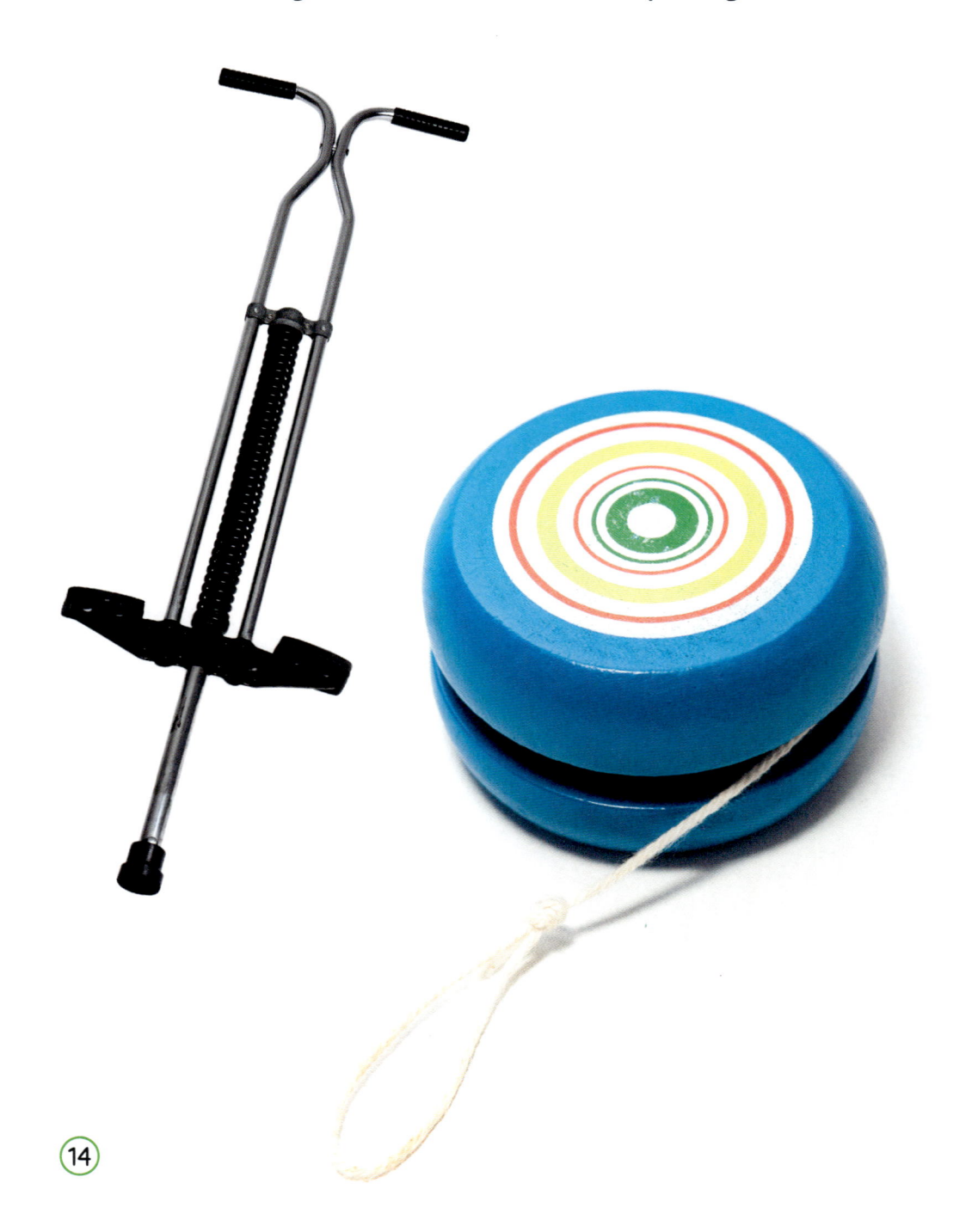

The spring in this toy is how it can go up and down. How long can you stay on?

Can you sort the words on this page into two groups?

Joy

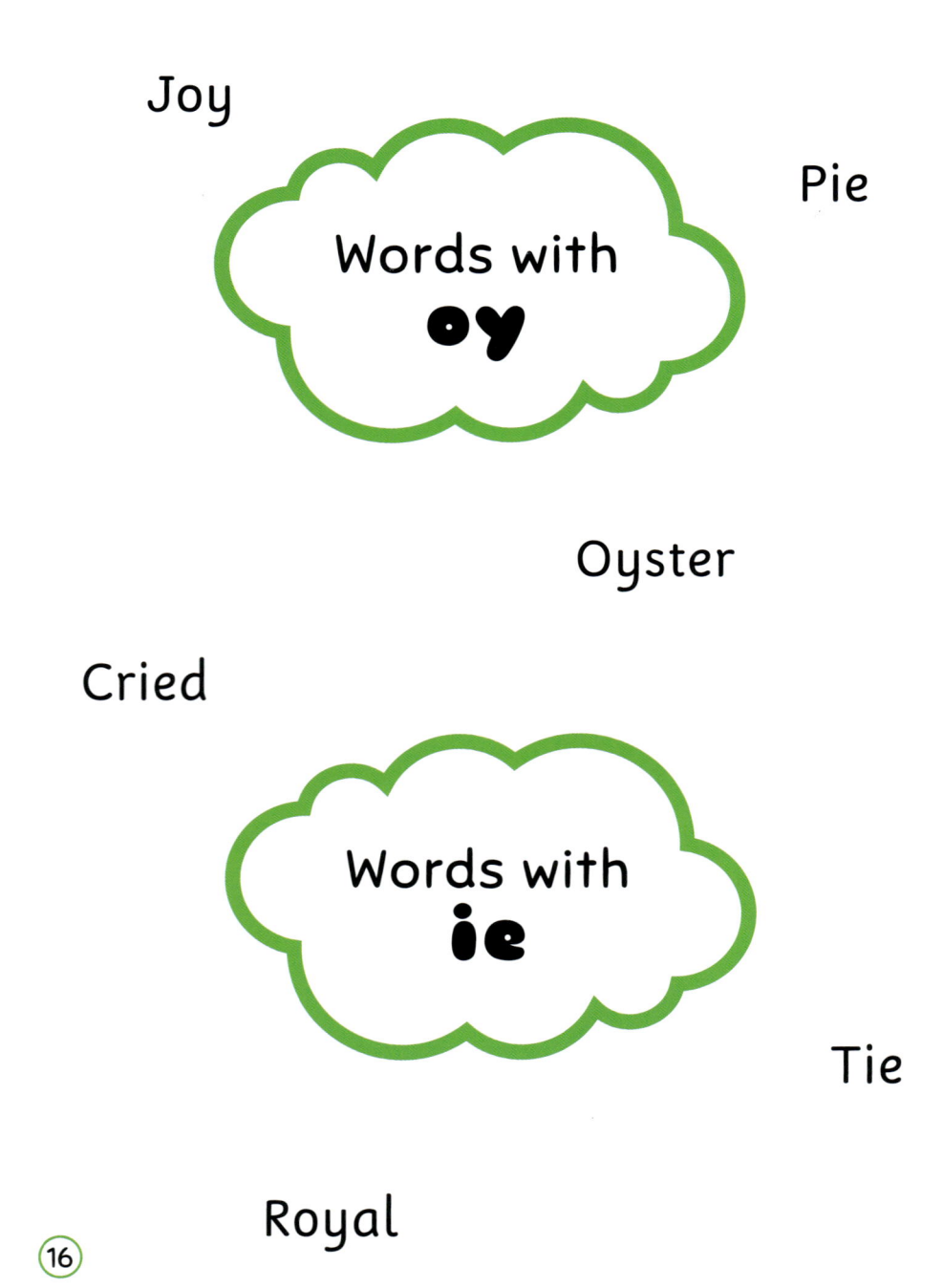

Pie

Words with **oy**

Oyster

Cried

Words with **ie**

Tie

Royal